The

Mohan Ramphal

ISBN 978-1-716-04329-1

Other books by Mohan Ramphal

- Bhagwad Gita
- Anthista Sanskar
- Wedding Handbook: Vivah Sanskar
- Nitya Pooja
- Organizational Compartmentalism
- Eight Steps to Achieve Enduring Peace and Happiness

Dedication

For my grandchildren Liam, Devina and Desmond.

Love.

Prologue

It was scorching hot on the 15th March, 2072, when they blasted off from the desert of Summerville. They knew very well that their Kundalini would be thoroughly disrupted for the next three months, but they were prepared to endure. Temporary disruption of bodily energy would fade in comparison to the pending microbial apocalypse from which they were trying to escape. As it turned out, exactly as planned, their capsule gracefully descended on the red desert which was sparkling bright, even from thirty-four million miles away.

"Operation Red Deer, this is mission control. Do you hear me? Over..."

"Mission Control, this is Red Deer–copy that. Over ..."

"Signing off at exactly 18 hours, 36 minutes and 44 seconds, over ..."

"Roger."

When Nicolas Sarkozie, Rawaana Ubantu, and Zing Lee stepped out from the elongated capsule onto the Martian surface, Ubantu couldn't control his amusement.

"Holy smokes!" he shouted. "This bloody place is cold, man! Who the heck in their right mind would think that *anything* could ever live here?"

"Hey bro, I'd say let's go in that direction," Lee agreed. "The way I look at it, it should be warmer over there."

"Okay, that's fine," Captain Sarkozie declared. "Let's do it."

The trio strapped all their gears and tobogganed down the dune with the speed of a two-wheel rover. Constantly they looked around to see from which direction the wind blew, but there was no breeze. So they just kept focused on their destination while they scrupulously looked out for rocks and boulders that scattered all over the place.

Without any clouds in the sky, sunlight was very slow to go away. To Lee, it looked like a very long day; '*too long*' he thought. Finally, when they found a really good spot, they set up their camp which will be their permanent home for the next five days. They could not light a campfire for sure; instead, they jerry-rigged a contraption to make some hot beverages and warm their hands.

"It sure is an interesting job to travel for one month to come here, just to dig a hole," said Ubantu, as they set up their telescope to begin their adventure.

"From what I've noticed so far, it looks like somebody's been here before us," Lee observed.

"Oh yeah," agreed Captain Sarkozie. "My grand-dad told me some very interesting stories about his mission here a long, long time ago."

"Then he might have known about those chariot tracks over there, I'd say," Lee suggested. "Captain, what do you know?"

"Oh boy, that's a very l-o-n-g story; that old man had all kinds of stories to tell brother, but this one I loved best"

Chapter One

A real boo-boo

From the clouds high up above it was a scenic and tranquil panoramic view. Lush greenery with tall trees and lakes flanked the outskirts of the city of Ramville. The raising fresh air purified the atmosphere and it was mesmerizing. Even the village houses appeared randomly arranged so that there were no fences between them. The city of Ramville was picturesque; it was *the* dreamland indeed.

All the inhabitants were roaming around freely without reservation. Even the King's son would hunt for sport and delicacies without escorts or guards. Some say that this place was the perfect *'heaven on earth'*.

The chirping of birds, laughter among neighbors and, playful sounds of children echoed in the far distance. Yet this summer paradise could be sultry sometimes when even the animals would resort to their sanctuaries as they would quietly await the arrival of the beautiful night sky.

One day Nemi, the only son of the old emperor, wandered off into the forest all by himself; he wanted to spend the day in a sporting hunt alone. Confident that he is mature in strength that he can command any situation at will, he galloped off into the woods without any Royal escorts whatsoever. The bank of the large lake was the perfect spot to hunt because that is where animals will have to go to escape the desert heat. To his surprise, it did not take him very long to realize that any catch would be very hard to find.

"I can't go back empty-handed," Nemi told himself. "It is unbecoming of me to be unsuccessful."

He took a deep sigh and planned a stealth tactic. He knew that he was a well-trained marksman who could shoot a target only by listening to the direction of its sound. Meticulously, he gathered a few twigs and branches and made himself a camouflage. Then blending seamlessly in the ravine next to the lake, he was sure that animals will eventually come there to take a drink.

For a long time, no animal came, and the eerie silence made him wonder if the forest itself had conspired against his sportive event. At last, he heard a ruffle that sounded like an elephant. Immediately he double-checked his arsenal of arrows which he had carefully packed together. There were some which were designed to kill and many more which were designed only to disable his catch.

"This one will do," he spoke to himself. Then he smelled it—just to make sure.

Nemi was well known as a person of great compassion and love. Not wanting to kill the object which he heard, he carefully fitted a special arrow to his bow. Then ensuring that he cannot be seen, he concentrated on the sound of the target. When he was satisfied that he will not miss, he pulled the string of the bow to his ear and let go the arrow with a mighty force. '*Swish*' he heard and then immediately the moaning cry of a person.

"Oh my god, what did I do?" he lamented. Frantically, he ran to the scene to rescue the target.

To his dilemma the target was not an elephant; it was a young boy who took the shot squarely on his chest. The prince tried desperately to remove the stuck arrow but he quickly realized that he cannot do so safely; Nemi was devastated. Confused, he tried to caress the victim. Just then he noticed by the name tag on the boy's shirt; that his name was Xhi.

"Is your name Xhi?" Nemi asked politely.

The boy did not reply, he just stared into space and moaned. When he muscled enough strength to speak he asked,

"Sir, who are you? What did I do for you to harm me like this?" Xhi sobbed profusely. "I, I, I am… only here… to, to dip some drinking water ....for my ailing parents."

The prince immediately became grief-stricken beyond his comprehension. His mouth was parched and he could not control his trembling. He gathered his thoughts and replied,

"My friend, my name is Nemi. I am a young prince of this land", he wiped his nose and sobbed. "I am here alone in this forest only on a sporting adventure."

He paused and gently stroked the forehead of the injured victim. "When I hid in the ravine, I heard a noise which I believed to be that of an elephant," Nemi shook his head. "So I shot my arrow. I beg you to forgive me; please…I swear I had no intention at all to hurt you."

The prince hugged the injured Xhi as if he was his birth brother; and wept like a child.

"It is my entire fault. I should have been more certain of the object before I shoot. I honestly beg your forgiveness. Please … please allow me to take this water to your parents for you."

With a weak hand, Xhi pointed in the direction of his parents. Then he slowly took a deep breath while in the arms of Nemi and closed his eyes.

Prince Nemi looked around frantically for someone to help, but no one else was there. Alone and helpless, he burst into a loud cry as he fell and buried his head between his knees.

"Oh my God, what am I supposed to do? How can I convey this unfortunate news to the parents of this lad?" Nemi mumbled to himself, as he laid the victim on the bank of the lake. "How can I convince them that it was all an accident? What will I say to them that will pacify their agony?"

He stopped for a moment and reflected that throughout his life as a prince, no one ever taught him how to follow instructions. Today, however, he has to follow his instructions.

"I constantly gave my servants instructions in the past, but I never knew how to perform them myself," he said to himself, and then he thoughtfully looked to the sky and froze. "As a person of Royal descent, I have a civic duty to my citizens. I will have to be honest about this whole incident and take responsibility for my action. Now I have to behave like their son, and try to mollify those grieving parents."

Nemi took the bowl which the Xhi was carrying, filled it with water from the lake, and proceeded to deliver it. When he was within audible distance of the old couple, he couldn't help but noticed that they were visibly blind and weak. Just then the old woman said,

"Oh my son, my heart is trembling, and I am having some kind of fear. I have a feeling that you are sad. You are unusually quiet my child, is something wrong?"

Out of dejection, the prince could not speak so he caressed the hand of the old woman. She in turn reached and touched his face.

She asked surprisingly, "Who are you? Where is my son?"

She fumbled the space around her trying to feel if Xhi is there. "Where is my son? Please tell me so that my fear can go away. Xhi, are you here? Why don't you speak to me, my child?"

"Oh mother, your son has been killed in a tragic accident ..."

"This cannot be!" yelled the old man who is now visibly upset. "Who has done this to our only child?" he shouted and clapped his hands. "Oh heavenly God, this pain is unbearable!"

He sobbed profusely and said, "Sir, I beg of you, please bring our son here so that we can feel and speak to him ourselves".

Nemi has torn himself, he knew that he had to offer his best comfort to the parents of the slain boy.

"Oh good father, your son cannot come because he is dead. It was me who shot the deadly arrow, holy Sir." Nemi panted. "I swear to you, dear father, his death is an accident. When I shot my arrow, I truly believed that it was a wild animal at which I was shooting."

The prince fell on his knees and begged. "Please accept me as your son dear parents; I will do everything you desire for your comfort. I beseech you — please understand that I too am affected by this whole tragedy."

"You are already the son of another mother, my child," replied the Xhi's mother. "Never in this world can you be our son —no, not in this world, Oh great one." She sobbed bitterly. "I held my child in my bosom when he was a baby. He suckled from me when I fed him from my own body," she cried. "Nobody can ever understand this feeling. We grew together. We were different bodies with the same soul." Then she remained quiet and sobbed.

She huffed and said, "Oh King, you will never be able to understand our needs, because you are a King and we are mere beggars."

"Today, we are childless ourselves," lamented Xhi's father. "In these last moments of our lives, we are saddened that we will die without our son at our side."

Everyone was completely silent. The long pause felt like a boring day.

"I say to you today Oh prince, a father without his son by his side in times of need, is like a horse that has only two legs; it cannot stand. Yes! I say *this father* is indeed weak without his son at his side. Today I am that unfortunate one; today I am doomed!"

The old man looked up to the sky, extended his hands, and bellowed: "In the same manner that today I will die without our son at my side, there will come a day when you also, Oh prince, will grieve for your son at the time of your death".

Both parents sobbed profusely in agitation. Then they sat motionlessly and stared at Nemi; and when their jaw dropped, he gently closed their eyes with his hands.

The entire forest was dreadfully quiet - even the waves in the lake disappeared. For the first time in his life, the young prince felt lonely. His mind was perturbed beyond his comprehension. He delicately gathered the three bodies and cremated them with as much dignity as he could, then he gracefully walked to his horse and slowly rode off in the distance.

"I can never relate this incident to anyone," he mumbled to himself. "If what the dying father of that innocent young man just said could ever be true, then I must have to learn to live and deal with his regret for the rest of my life."

Chapter Two

Nemi met his wife

The past two years in Ramville went by in a jiffy. Although prince Nemi was actively engaged in royal duties, he always remembered the unfortunate incident of the young man whom he shot in the forest. This made him extra scrupulous in everything that he did. Whenever he became disturbed, he would practice martial arts to control his mind and his emotions. In due course of time, he became almost invincible in archery and combat. Soon he became very much loved by the citizens of the kingdom, and he became very caring to everyone.

Nemi was forty years old when his father suddenly became terminally ill and he knew that he will inherit the kingdom after his father pass away. His responsibilities to nationhood became more complex, especially when he visited the villages and towns and had difficulty relating to the daily lives of those who were socially challenged.

"Sir, if you will ever understand their situations, you will have to live like them," one of his senior ministers advised him.

As time went by, Nemi studied the art of governing. Then on a beautiful July day, he heard of a special event that will be taking place in the neighboring kingdom of Kosal. There the king will attempt to find a husband for his daughter. Nemi was open to the concept of *'match-making'* because he always schooled that spousal relationships are predestined by some higher celestial authority.

In preparation to attend the program, he reflected on the deadly mistake that happened when he traveled alone and shot an innocent boy in the forest. Determined that he will not make any silly mistake again, he took a group of dedicated confidants with him in high hopes that he will be victorious in winning the hand of the king's daughter.

From miles away the young prince could hear the sound of Flutes and Kittle Drums; they were tantalizing to say the least. The whole atmosphere was filled with a peculiar aroma of food. All the streets were decorated with welcoming flowers and ornaments. Men and women were dressed in beautiful traditional suites;

everyone seemed to be dancing when they walked towards the King's palace.

"Hey, a prince is coming!" yelled a young girl.

"Yes, he must be very rich!" shouted another, as she jumped up and down. "Look at the army who are his company."

Just then a few teenage village boys ran ahead of Nemi's procession and shouted at the top of their lungs to everyone: "Prince Nemi is coming! Prince Nemi is coming! And he has lots of people with him!"

Nemi looked stunningly elegant in his royal outfit as he slowly rode and lead the procession on his white steed. Residents of the town frantically ran and formed rows of witnesses on both sides of the road. The crowd cheered and waved their hats as the procession marched along.

Another horseman from a nearby kingdom was also attended by the invitation of the king of Kosal. When he saw Nemi's procession, he noticed the prince on his horse and thought to himself, "I am not the only horseman around here today. It sure looks fun is already in the air."

He rode up beside Nemi and smiled.

Nemi acknowledges with a nod.

"So…, you are here to try to win the hand of the young maiden, eh?"

"Yes of course. And you?"

The visitor raised his eyebrows and shook his head. "We are both in this together pal," he said with a wide smile.

As they continue to ride along, the horseman couldn't help but marvel at the grand welcome that the citizens were performing. People were cheering and throwing flowers on the road as if they were honoring their guests royally.

"This looks like a royal welcome," he said to Nemi.

They both laughed quietly.

"Well my friend, this is great! I was not expecting this at all," he continued. "I think either you are a prince, or I am."

"Well, one of us sure is," Nemi chuckled.

There were crowds of people that were gathered everywhere when they entered the palace. Some were entertained by dancers dressed in colorful attire; others had a ring-side view of friendly wrestling matches where young men displayed their muscular physique and physical authority over the others. Eventually, a chubby gentleman, who was dressed in traditional peacock feathers' head-gear, sounded a big drum that hung over his broad chest.

"Can I have your attention everyone? he shouted. "The King of Kosal has ordered that the ceremony of finding a suitor for his precious daughter, Kosaler, must begin immediately".

The royal guards sounded their horns and trumpets while the marching band saluted the King and his family as they took their respective royal seats. Then, blending their voices, the royal quartet sang in perfect harmony various songs that Nemi never heard of before. All that he could remember was what he *thought* he heard. He hummed:

"...*Vala lala lala, vala vala,*
Hmm, hmmm, hmmm
We must be kind, let there be love..."

Then when big drum sounded again, and the master of ceremony announced, "The King has ordered that whoever, with one arrow, could pierce the eye of the fish hanging on this pole above — without looking at the fish, that hero will win the hand of his beautiful daughter." He paused and looked around.

"I will place a bowl of water directly below the target. All contestants must only look at the reflection of the target in the water; then he must shake the bowl and shoot before the ripples settled. You will be disqualified if you ever look directly at the target."

The crowd grunted aloud and every contestant looked at the other beside him.

"That is impossible!" said one.

13

"Is he trying to embarrass us or what? I say we go spend our time in the bar, for heaven's sake," replied someone else.

The big drum rolled again and the M.C. waived his index finger and continued, "Whoever fails to shoot the target in a single try will humiliate their kingdom and themselves. They will not–I repeat will not be served with any delicacy, and they must leave without even looking at the princess."

Prince Nemi surveyed the crowd and saw all the strong men hanging their heads. He cracked his neck and muttered, "This is not a contest about the show of strength; it is about the show of discipline." In deep contemplation, he thanked his yoga teacher for the tough training that he had to endure during his formative years.

When it was his turn to enter the contest, Nemi stood below the pole of the hanging fish. He remembered the incident when he shot Xhi in the forest and reflected on how dejected he was.

"I truly wish I could have reversed that fatal arrow and saved that innocent man's life," he mumbled. "Oh well, I can't erase the past, but if could ever do something to liberate that man's soul, that would be a small step in my redemption."

He looked at the master of ceremony and asked, "Before I shoot my arrow, Sir, may I request that you turn the fish around so that I could see the other eye please?"

"What difference does it make, mister?"

"I don't want to look at *'that'* eye Sir; I desire to look at the other one please."

A servant approached the King and whispered in his ear. The King nodded. The servant then approached the master of ceremony and gesticulated to him.

"Very well dear prince, we will turn the target around for you," the master of ceremony consented.

As the target was being turned around, Nemi prayed. *"Dear God, today I beg of you to forgive my sin of slaying that innocent child in the forest. If you bless me enough Oh Lord, I will also win the prize of my life today. Sweet Lord, would you please let this moment be the day of change in my life."*

With confidence in his mind, the prince bowed and touched the pole with the hanging target, and then he strung an arrow to his bow. In deep concentration, he looked at the rippled water and saw the fish's eye which was as bright as a full moon.

"What is he doing?" whispered someone in the audience.

"Shhh!" whispered another. "Ha, he must be a mystic of some sort!"

Nemi's concentration was unwavering, there he saw in a split moment, an object appeared as a reflection in the target's eye—it was a person with an arrow sticking out of his chest, but Nemi could only see the object from behind. The concentration of the prince was so intense that for a moment he felt like he levitated off the ground. Just then he discharged the arrow from his bow. In his imagination, the stuck arrow from the person's chest suddenly ejected like a shooting star and disappeared.

"Bull's eye!" yelled the crowd.

Others shouted, "Fish eye!"

"Long live the prince! Long live Prince Nemi!" cried his entourage of supporters.

Then the King of Kosal smiled and arose from his throne. Everyone in the palace also stood in silence.

After a few hours, the prince was ushered into a special chamber. He looked around in admiration as he was surrounded by an array of royal servants. He did not even see when his clothes were removed; he only knew that he was wearing just an undergarment on his waist. Nemi didn't remember his feet touching the floor before he was placed on a specially decorated stool where a host of senior women anointed his body with special oils and fragrances.

"This one is very good for you," one of the older ladies said, pointing to a small green bottle.

"Smell this," said another. "This on will chase away any evil spirits," she assured him.

'I can't smell anything,' Nemi thought to himself with a smile. *'My head is spinning around.'*

Another lady mixed some herbs in a wooden cup, stirred it a few times, and almost forced him to drink it.

"We call this *'goochee'*; you should drink this every day. It is very, very good for your back," she said with a cynical smile. "I should know; I have seven children, yes s-e-v-e-n!" she said, showing one hand with wide opened fingers.

That evening, the wedding ceremony of Prince Nemi and princess Kosaler was splendidly attended. The jubilation was tantalizing, and most of the young boys appeared to be unable to stand still or walk in a straight line. Along the aisle leading up to the wedding tent, there were complimentary figurines of exotic animals and the entire wedding hall itself was beautifully decorated with yellow and white roses.

One of his guards said to him, "Do you notice, Your Highness? They know that you have a close affiliation with the Sun God; that's why they specially select yellow roses for you."

"Where are the balloons?" asked one village child.

"They did not put them up honey," her mommy replied.

"But why, mommy?"

"They're afraid this guy might shoot them down with his eyes!" her brother chuckled.

The jubilation was loud and young men were staggering when they walked; it was difficult to understand the gibberish which they were speaking and the whole celebration was a huge masquerade. When the music was paused long enough, the priest asked Nemi, "Do you take this bride to be your wedded wife?"

"I do." He pumped his chest with pride.

"Do you take this groom as your wedded husband?"

"I do," she replied bashfully.

"Cheers!" the crowd bellowed. "Yes, it's over — it's party time!"

The King's guards blew their celebratory trumpets and horns as if they announced some kind of national victory. Even the dancing and singing among the audience was exuberant.

"They are truly a perfect couple!" everyone in attendance was saying among themselves.

The King ordered a battalion of guards and a massive marching band of royal musicians to escort the bride and groom away when they left the kingdom of Kosal.

"*Hmm, I came on one horse. Now I am leaving on a horse-cart AND a bride,*" Nemi thought to himself, as the newlyweds elegantly rode off into the distance in a beautiful white chariot.

When they reached the border of Ramville, Nemi's army was equally decorated and receptive. The streets were elegantly decorated with imported flowers and earthen lamps flanked the pathway to the King's throne.

Chapter Three

The birth of Harmony

When Nemi's father passed away shortly after his marriage, he inherited the kingdom and became King of Ramville; princess Kosaler was also crowned as the queen as well. The entire country noticed that from the onset the new King was a very kind, forgiving, and loving monarch. He treated everyone with due respect, and in turn, they also reciprocated the same to him and the royal family. Everyone in the city appeared happy. Living in Ramville was extremely delightful for the young bride. She loved the outdoors and had a curious admiration for the natural beauty of the various flower gardens. One beautiful evening Queen Kosaler and some of her maids went on a countryside stroll to enjoy the fall scenery.

"This whole country is truly heaven on earth," she said to one of her closest attendants.

The maid replied, "Yes, Your Highness. And you know what?" she looked around and point. "There are no policemen in this city either!"

"WOW! How do the citizens barter and trade?"

"Everybody lives off the land ma'am," said the maid, as she pointed to a large patch of garden which was occupied by a small group of peasants.

"That's a very large family!" the Queen commented. She was certain that she understood the social concept.

"No ma'am," replied the maid with a smile. 'They are all neighbors. Working as a community means that no task is too difficult for anyone to tackle."

"But what if someone wants something that the other doesn't?"

"Ma'am, the general philosophy of our culture is that anything beyond our needs is considered an attachment," the maid humbly explained. "Eventually, attachments become bondage, and in bondage, we cannot live as freely as we would have otherwise wished."

The Queen bit her lips and nodded.

The maid continued, "Look at the birds and the animals, there is no competition among them. They seem happy, right?"

Queen Kosaler glanced at the trees and the animals and smiled. In the brief moment of silence, she thought to herself, *"This lady is organically genuine; I think I can keep her as a trusted confidant."*

The maid also felt their camaraderie; she relaxed her shoulders with a slight exhale.

"Tell me, do you know what *'goochee'* is?" the Queen asked. "The King mentioned it a few times to me, but it doesn't sound right ...I mean I don't know what it is." She shimmered and gesticulated in her unique girly style, "The word itself doesn't sound right, does it?"

"No, I don't think so, I never heard of it myself."

"Oh well, you know men! They don't remember anything, they never know what they're talking about, and they surely don't have a-n-y clue what's in the kitchen!" Kosaler laughed.

They both giggled amiably the whole evening. They ended their evening stroll with laughter as each resorted to their respective quarters in the royal palace.

It was hardly two years since their marriage when a beautiful girl baby was born of King Nemi and Queen Kosaler; she was named *'Harmony'* by their spiritual master.

"Your husband is a very friendly person," he told the Queen during the naming ceremony. "You are a very beautiful lady. The birth star of this child is such that she inherits divine qualities from you and your husband. I foretell that she will bring happiness to others by her sheer presence alone."

King Nemi was gratefully happy about the birth of his daughter. He was confident that his marriage to Queen Kosaler was divine intervention. First, it liberated the soul of the slain young man when he shot the fish's eye, and now he knows that the curse of Xhi's father won't come true. He contemplated that he can continue his life without duress because *God* is on his side.

With every passing day, little princess Harmony grew even prettier; other children in her kindergarten loved her too. Anywhere she went, she constantly received gifts and good wishes from elders and the general population. Life in the kingdom of Ramville was flourishing with peace, joy, and happiness.

News of this paradise quickly reached the neighboring states and soon the entire continent was emulating the statehood of the Nemi's kingdom. He was constantly having frequent visitors from near and far— many of them uninvited.

On a cool breezy day, one of his old schoolmates visited him impromptuly. The royal gatekeeper ran to the king to convey the news that a particular visitor was waiting outside to meet him.

"Your majesty, there is mendicant waiting outside the compound. He said is desirous to speak to you in person," reported the servant.

"I am not aware of any such royal coming to meet me," the king replied. "But if you assess the situation and you believe that it is safe for me to do so, of course, let him in."

There were no kittle drums or celebratory trumpets for the lone visitor. He approached the King's palace only with quiet footsteps. His slim frame flanked by fully grown salt-and-pepper bearded, Nemi did not remember him at first, but as soon as he offered his greetings, the King recognized him instantly.

Nemi stepped off his throne and with sincere humility, he received his visitor with open arms in the most cordial way was as he could. Without saying a word, the king ushered him a seat next to his throne. Queen Kosaler looked at the King admirably and thought to herself:

"How could anyone not like this man? He is so powerful yet so loving and humble."

The King placed his hand on the shoulder of his friend and spoke to Kosaler. "Do you see your Highness? This is my childhood friend, *Lompa*. As children, we played together, ate together, and slept together. After our formative years, we departed in our separate ways."Nemi fought back tears and swallowed.

He continued, "It is because of YOU that he is here to visit me again."

"Oh no, Your Honor, it is not me at all; it is because of *your* fame that he comes to visit you."

Later that evening after a sumptuous banquet, the King entertained his friend in personal conversations.

"So, how have you been and how are my sister-in-law and the other family members?" he asked cordially.

"Everyone is doing very well," Lompa replied. "Our house is not as jubilant as yours though."

"What, is there tension within the family?"

"Oh no, not at all; it's just that we don't have children," Lompa said with dejection. "By the will of Nature, we can't either."

"Do you ever heard of *'goochee'*?" Nemi asked.

Not wanting to appear as if he is naïve, Lompa replied with great confidence, "Is that the brown stuff with six legs which we just had? Yea, I'd say it didn't taste too bad."

"Oh, ha-ha; you are still very funny!" Nemi burst into a cynical laugh. "Okay, Okay, alright! Did you discuss this with your advisors and so on?"

"No." Lompa shook his head. "What's the point?"

"Okay. Relax, let me ask my elders this evening and see if they have any suggestions to offer," Nemi assured him.

Later that evening as the royal couple went to bed, the King was noticeably in deep contemplation.

"You don't look very well," Kosaler enquired. "Did you have too much to eat today?"

"No, I'm just thinking about my friend Lompa...poor man!"

"What about him that is so disturbing?"

"Kosh, a home with a child must be a very desolate place to live," he huffed. He always called her 'Kosh' because to him 'she looks more beautiful with that name'.

"There is nothing wrong with that; besides we can't do anything about it, can we?" she asked.

"Well... the ancients and the philosophers always say that great happiness is derived from helping others," Nemi stated resourcefully.

"Okay then." She folded her arms then tapped her cheek. "As part of our marriage vows, I had promised to support you in 'any endeavors either at home or abroad'. Whatever you decide, it will be Ok with me."

The King folded his arms and paused for a moment.

"Maybe we can let him adopt our child," he said soberly.

The Queen reacted to the sudden jolt she felt in her knees. Her chest pumped erratically, and then she rolled her eyes and collapsed on the bed. Nemi saw that there was an obvious sign of lactation on her bust line. He felt a bit dejected, but quickly he regained his composure and thought, "*I did it again.*" As often, his general good nature seemed to have control over his judgment.

He crouched over and stroked her forehead gently.

"Oh no-no-no, I don't mean that he should take our child away! Not at all, that's NOT what I meant," he reassured her softly. "I just meant to say that he could consider and spent some time with her just as if she is his daughter."

"But what if their bond grows stronger and she eventually wants to go and live with him? What if..."

"Oh don't be silly! The bond between mother and child can never be broken," he philosophized stepping backward. "They say that such bond is so strong, even God cannot understand it."

The Queen did not reply.

"Oh yeah," he continued, "I heard that even the *big guy* up there can be confused in these situations once-in-a-while." He tried to cheer her up.

"Alright," she droops her shoulders. "I trust you. Promise that we will not lose our child?"

The King showed her his pinky finger then touched his heart and smiled. "I'll allow them to just acquaint themselves and see how it goes."

King Lompa and young Princes Harmony often played in the courtyard of Ramville. Within days she started to address him as *"Huncle Loma."* Soon the bond between them grew stronger. Eventually, she was allowed to visit his kingdom and return home to Ramville for a few days.

In due course in time, Lompa started to take the young princess to her school. By the time she was a teenager her absence from Queen Kosaler and King Nemi became a thing of the past; everyone accepted that Princess Harmony was the adopted daughter of King Lompa.

Chapter Four

Nemi's marriage to Pricilla

It has been ten years since Princess Harmony went to live with King Lompa permanently; Nemi and Kosaler were empty nesters once again. They were reluctant to bring their child back to their home because they were concerned that the child would have become distressed and sad. Of course, both kings did not want to make *their* beloved child discourage, so they endured.

One day as Nemi was presiding over state matters; it dawn upon him that he will have to vacate the throne someday.

"But whom will I pass this kingdom to?" he consulted with his senior ministers during a confidential family discussion.

"Don't worry Oh King, it is already ordained that you will have sons," his most senior minister, Jo-ji, told him.

"However, Queen Kosaler might not be their birth mother," he predicted.

Although they were the Royal rulers, the King and Queen would never disregard the wisdom of senior ministerial members. These men and women possessed divine wisdom which was given to them when celestial angels visited the kingdom during auspicious times. Therefore, it is expected that they would verbalize their thoughts only after deep meditation and introspection.

Nemi and Kosaler pondered on the prediction for a few days, until one evening when they were on an evening stroll, he said to her, "It could probably be very true what Jo-ji predicted, you know; but how?"

It was not unusual for kings to have multiple wives, so Nemi and Queen Kosaler mutually agreed that if he would ever co-habit with another wife, she — Kosaler, will remain as the senior wife with supervisory powers.

In due course in time, King Nemi adopted '*Pricilla*' as his new wife. Being the daughter of a popular merchant from another country did not impede her piety. She was witty, beautiful, and flamboyant; she was the ideal companion to spice up the life of the aging king.

During one daily briefing of the legislator, a senior member of the king's council reported that the gods and demons were engaged in a fierce battle, and the gods desperately needed the King's help to win the war.

"Why would the gods require ME to help them?" enquired Nemi.

"Sir, you are well known in the entire universe for your skill in archery," the minister reminded him. "The gods in the heavens are fully aware of your military might and the depth of your scientific achievements."

He walked to the center of the podium and continued, "They witnessed the unique task which you performed to win the hand of our Queen Kosaler, Oh King. They are convinced that if anyone can enhance the natural powers of the world to help their cause dear Sir, it would be you."

"Very well," replied Nemi. "Have our military vehicles prepared, inspected, and ready."

"Yes Sir!" the minister salutes.

"Look here — pay special attention to my chariot."

When the news reached the Queens' chambers, Pricilla and Kosaler discussed how they can contribute to helping their husband in his endeavor.

Pricilla said, "Your Highness, during the absence of the king, I suggest that you should stay in the kingdom to rule over the citizens. You are older, wiser, and are most perfect for this duty."

Kosaler twirled somewhat reserved and replied, "I believe that we should both stay back. I think the responsibilities would be much easier to manage."

"This is a dangerous war. Who would be by his side if ever he needs help?" plead the younger queen. "Besides-- I am younger, healthier, and just a little more agile," she said with a smile.

Queen Kosaler returned the smile and nodded in agreement.

At sunrise, the next morning King Omni and Queen Pricilla left the palace in their armored vehicle, along with a small contingent of soldiers.

"Why are we leaving so early?" she asked.

"It is the bright half of the moon phase," replied Nemi. "Legend has it that the angels come out of their dens to feast during this period. Just in case we need help in battle, I am sure they will offer their divine assistance."

Kosaler and her maids had prepared hot beverages and snacks for Nemi and Pricilla, but the King did not take any with him; instead, he took a quick sip and a few quick bites, the kissed her on her cheek.

"Is that it?" she asked. "I have all these wonderful delicacies specially made just for you, enough to last you three days, and this is all you'll take? May be...."

"You know Kosh, it's a jungle out there; it won't be fun," he assured her. "We might not even have time to rest our butts, much less to party."

Kosaler stared at Omni and realized that she can't win the discussion. She glanced at Pricilla and said, "Take this," she pointed to a pitcher of water. "You may need it — just in case."

The Royal bugle sounded the war command and the big drum called everyone to ease. All the horses were perfectly harnessed and tethered to their respected wagons, each carrying the flags of Ramville. All the soldiers were indeed pumped and ready to go. Leading the brigade was King Nemi himself. Pricilla operated the binoculars and compass, and it was she who raised the flag and commanded, "Let's go! Follow the King."

Nemi and his army had just entered the outskirts of the palace when the thunderous noise of war drums could be heard. Over the hills and behind the grey clouds for dust, the King saw that the battle between the gods and the demons was indeed very fierce. The gods were outnumbered as bullets, spears, and arrows were thrown at them from multiple sources.

Some of the gods were noticeably exhausted and their resistance to the demons was completely inadequate. Many of them were even running away, to his surprise. Nemi decided to enter the battle without negotiations. He ordered his army to advance forcefully.

"Quickly, follow me everyone!" he shouted.

"You, you and you—go to the east!" he commanded. "Hey, you…! Everybody follow this general!"

The intensity of the combat was breathtaking. Injured soldiers were being run over mercilessly by machines of all kinds. Those close to their opponents threw rocks at each other. Some uprooted trees; while others slammed their enemies' heads so viciously with their clubs that death was the only sure thing. Men were screaming and the bellowing of dying animals was deafening to Queen Pricilla, but she kept close to the king in their vehicle to help spot any incoming missiles. Suddenly, the King was attacked so violently that he took flight. Just about then a missile struck the wheel of their vehicle.

"Oh shit, duck! Go on, go on!" yelled Pricilla. "Don't stop, don't stop, I get this. Hurry, let's get out of here!"

To prevent the wheel from falling off, she stuck her figure into the hole of the axle that supported it. Eventually, they retreated to safety below a large tree, but only for a short time.

"I will always remember this courageous effort of yours to save my life today, my dear Pricilla," Nemi said to her. "Listen carefully my love; I make a solemn oath to you right here and now: *If at any time you desire something… anything, I will fulfill your wishes no matter what. This is my solemn promise to you."* He embraced and kissed her on top of her head.

Thereafter, when they sat for a drink of water from the pitcher which Kosaler gave her, Pricilla placed a damped rag on the forehead of the Nemi and tapped it gently. Then he looked at her and commented, "Behind a brave man, there is always a brave woman… "

"No, No," she interjected, "*Besides* — not behind."

"Alright, alright, Okay, you win; you know what I meant, right?"

As soon as he was rested briefly, he repaired his vehicle with an advanced sophisticated contraption which he had constructed during his spare time in the palace. Nobody knew that Nemi was a home-grown technical genius. Only the gods knew that during some nights, he had visited distant planets and stars. He was indeed '*a master of the skies*' they surmised.

Now fully armed and equipped, the King re-entered the battlefield with lightning speed and power. The demon army attacked him more forcefully than before, but he was able to avoid and defeat them from all directions.

"How the hell can he do that?" cried one of the enemies.

"For the devil's sake, he is moving in *all* ten directions!" another exclaimed.

"What are ten directions, anyways?" enquired someone.

"Liked this," a senior enemy soldier explained. He drew a circle in the sand, pointed, and said, "Lad, this is called *'On-the-job training'*, Okay? You only learn this once, don't you ever forget this... Here is the East, West, North, South..., North-East, North-West, South-East, and South-West."

"Yeah, but that's only eight," a young soldier stated.

"There is also UP and Down," the senior soldier continued.

They all froze and looked confused.

"I guess this means that we are done. Our demise is eminent," another concluded.

"It is impossible for us to discharge weapons in ALL directions at the same time. But we MUST persevere," the chief told them. "A soldier must conquer and defend. Living and dying are consequential in this job my friends; it is your duty, his duty... our duty to obey the command of our king and fight in this war." Then he commanded, "Come on, let's go boys, ATTACK!"

Although the demons attacked the king with all their might, he evaded them with his dexterity and skill. His vehicle was swishing around gyroscopically in every direction and his attackers were unable to precisely shoot at him. In their opinion, the King's vehicle was randomly swirling around like a *flying saucer*. The gods in heaven hailed praises unto Nemi as he vanquished his foes one after the other. Then they spoke in their heavenly voice, "FROM TODAY, YOU WILL FOREVER BE KNOWN IN THIS ENTIRE WORLD AS THE GREAT KING - *'OMNI'*."

News of Nemi's victory quickly reached the kingdom of Ramville, and all across the world. The celebration of his return was exuberant and grand. His subjects received him not only as a Royal, but also as a god, and they loved his new name - *'Omni'*. They swept the road before he walked and showered him with flowers and praises. Dancing, merriment, and jubilation were happening as far as the King could see.

When the King entered his palace and Queen Kosaler greeted him with warmth and love, he whispered to her, "This celebration outside fail in comparison to that of the day when *we* get married."

In due course in time, he explained to her the brave act of Queen Pricilla which saved his life. Kosaler complimented the junior Queen and saio to her, "I believe that we could live like true sisters and enjoy the King as our dreariest friend."

Two years passed since the Great War; again the kingdom of Ramville was beaming with life and prosperity. King Omni however, was visibly concerned about this age and the fact that he did not have a son who could become his heir.

"This is an important matter that should be addressed very soon;" he thought to himself. He planned to discuss it with his wives during their next dinner.

"What can we do to ensure that the Royal lineage is maintained?" he asked his queens.

"It might be a good idea to seek the counsel of our more senior and confidential minister," they replied in one voice.

Within hours the senior minister was summoned to advise the Royals on this important subject. When they convened, the minister explained candidly that he had no clue on how to solve this problem.

"I would require a few days to contemplate on this issue, Your Highness," he requested. "Only then would I be able to present you with any meaningful solution."

The king consented and later, it was obvious that he was more delightful than when he left their last discussion a few days ago.

"I suppose you have some good news for us, Sir," Omni enquired.

"Yes my Lord," was the causal reply as he placed his thumb on his lips.

"Sir, I humbly suspect that the gods will be glad to return a favor to you, on account of your help in defeating the demons during the Great War, but you must ask."

Everyone paused for a moment.

"I have been told," he continued, "that on the ninth day following the full moon in March *next* year, there will be a mystical alignment of the heavenly stars."

Then he raised his eyebrows and continued, "According to my calculations Oh King, this event is so odd, that it only occurs once every eighteen million years! In my telepathy and mediation, I saw that this circumstance is divinely ordained for the benefit of the world."

By the dint of his scientific intuition, King Omni shook his head in understanding. He said, "As always, we have deep faith in your foresight and wisdom. Your command Sir will be ours to obey."

The counselor continued, "Oh Great King, with the addition of lovely Queen Pricilla to your companionship, your life has become the epitome of true family values. Her demeanor and poise are seen by everybody as the perfect recipe for peace, love, and happiness in a family; everyone Sir is trying to emulate you."

Pricilla lowered her eyes and smiled bashfully, as Kosaler complimented her by tapping on the back.

The Minister glanced at the King and told him confidently, "Sir, you are well known in the whole world for your valor and piety; maybe, just maybe, you are the chosen beneficiary of this galactic interstellar mystery."

Together with his wives, King Omni thanked their Chief Minister and gave him many gifts—his buggy could hardly carry them all.

After a few weeks, the King and Queens embarked on a six-month charity spree. They traveled all over the country and offered various gifts to all the subjects in the kingdom—their sincere hope was that the collective good wishes of everyone will inspire the gods even more to satisfy the King's desire of having a son as his successor.

Chapter Five

The birth of sons

The ninth day of the moonlight week of March was indeed peaceful and unusually calm. The high blue sky over the kingdom was sparingly dotted with puffs of pure white clouds. The chirping of birds and the gaming of cats and dogs were delightful to watch. Even small bunnies hopped around as if they were the *kings of the land*. All the royal servants were in their respective quarters while King Omni was writing in his diary about his experience when he visited Mars.

"Congratulations, congratulations!" was the echoing screaming in the palace hallways. "A boy child is born of Queen Kosaler!"

"Queen Pricilla also has a wonderful baby son!" yelled another servant.

"Hurry….hurry! They are twins. No, no they are boys! Rush….go and inform the King immediately," someone shouted.

When the King heard the news he pushed his diary aside, sprang to his feet, and dashed for the door; then he crashed into it and laughed at himself. As he frantically ran through the hallways, he was missing the chambers as he was opening doors randomly like a lost child in a maze. Eventually, the door of Kosaler's room flew open, King Omni stood frozen like a mannequin at the royal boutique.

"Please come in," spoke the Queen softly as she extended her hands.

Omni did not reply. He staggered towards the baby, extended his arms, and cried: "Alas! Thank you, God, my son is here."

Queen Kosaler was baffled for a moment. For the first time, she was in the company of another person and the King did not notice her.

"I am feeling very well too, you know!" she said faintly with a smile.

"Oh, I know, but look at him, Kosh! Isn't he gorgeous?" He held the baby's hands, "Sweet little hands, sweet little feet, beautiful curly hair! Look at his innocent eyes! This has to be the handy work of the gods," he said confidently.

Kosaler smiled. "I am sure he will grow up to become brave and handsome just as you are," she replied.

Just then some other maid servants wheeled Queen Pricilla and her baby to the room where the King was. Both queens were overwhelmed with emotions as they spoke at length about their experiences; the King though was speechless. He was constantly looking at both babies and at times appeared confused as to which one is whose.

In the presence of everyone who was there, one of the more senior maid servants, who always walked with a cane, suddenly barged into the queen's chamber. She stood in the middle — between the babies and the King.

She confronted him in a grandmotherly fashion, "You are NOT supposed to look at them as yet. These mothers have to show the children the sun god first. HE makes everything, so HE is their real father."

Everybody chuckled.

"It's OK Eva, their father already offered compliments to the gods," Pricilla interjected.

Eva was an older maid servant who was a personal assistant to Queen Pricilla. Everybody says that she is always grumpy because she was never married and never had children of her own. Most of the young girls in the palace did not like her; because to them, she is always bossy. There are even rumors that she once strangled a baby. Some say that on cold full moon nights, she darts around the palace riding on a broom stick. Pricilla however, knew that none of those allegations were true and always treated her with motherly respect. Eva was the queen's most trusted confidant.

"*She has age and experience,*" Pricilla once told the king about Eva.

"*Yeah, but experience is good-- depending on how it's used,*" he told her.

The next day, the senior councilor was once again summoned to assist the King and Queens in finding 'good names' for their children. Anticipating that his role will be demanding, as usual, the councilor took with him some pebbles in his pouch.

"Holy Sir, we beseech to help us find suitable names for our beloved children," the King requested.

"Of course, my Lord."

The minister folded his arms and nodded. Methodically, he placed the pebbles on the table in front of him. Then with a strange hand motion, he mystically arranged them while whispering something.

"*He is saying his secret password,*" whispered Kosaler to Pricilla.

"Kosaler's child should be named *Jay* and Pricilla's child should be named *Mariyaad,*" announced the minister. "This older brother will grow up to become a true statesman, and his younger brother will follow him very closely. Mariyaad will also be the more empathetic of the two. In fact, they both will be renowned throughout the whole world for their discipline and no-nonsense approach; men and women will sing their praises for as long as the sun shines and trees grow."

The great sigh of relief and sense of joy emanating from the King's chamber resonated to the end of the universe. As usual, jubilation filled the streets of Ramville in the blink of an eye.

"Thank you Oh Holy One! My internal fear and agitation have been removed," Omni told the minister.

"We too Oh great father, are extremely grateful to you for your benedictions and guidance," the Queens followed.

Eva was present there also, but she was completely unemotional. She glance at the children and took a long look at Jay as if she missed the entire ceremony.

The children grew up under strict parental supervision until they were ten years old, which was the mandatory age for higher education- according to the King's tradition. As such, they were sent off to a specialized homeopathic-yoga school that was renowned for its quality of education. The teacher was so good that past students and parents alike gave him the nickname "*Yogi*". Under his guidance, the brothers bonded with many kids from other privileged families, but they were exceptional as they were often regarded as seniors in their class.

"The first and most important lesson in life," their preceptor told them, "is to understand your selves but from within. This knowledge about your '*inner self*' is a secret."

"Does this means that we'll have to become doctors?" asked one of the kids from the back of the class.

Yogi laughed and said, "My son, the external world is a projection of yourself. You MUST understand this philosophy."

"And what if we don't?" asked Mariyaad.

"Isn't it true that living aloof and being totally introspective is dilapidating to our personal growth?" asked Jay.

"No, not really: living in solitude will increase your foresight, but only in a certain way. To foster your growth, you will have to participate in community activities and put these and similar disciplines into action for the common good of all the people in your lives. That is how you must grow up!"

"How do we even begin?" enquired Jay.

"Simple: by taking good care of the environment and the earth, of course.

He turned to the other children and said, "Kids, you must always be mindful of your waste and your taste. If you pollute your environment, it will pollute you back. Now, *that* won't be funny."

"Is this a difficult thing to do?" asked Mariyaad.

"No, not at all. You should work smart, not hard."

"What do you mean, teacher Yogi?" asked another child.

"Very simple," said the instructor. "Come here, let me show you. Go to the kitchen and bring a fruit, -any fruit."

The young man rushed into the kitchen of the dormitory and brought a handful of cherries.

"Now eat one and give five to any five of your friends," instructed Yogi. "Each of you must eat your fruit and then plant the seeds at different spots."

Each student followed the instruction diligently and scattered their seeds randomly, and reported back to their teacher as they were required to do. To their surprise, teacher Yogi instructed them to dig up all the seeds again. However, they cannot complain, because they knew very well that if they do, their parents will be very upset with them when their report card is complied.

"Now," teacher Yogi said, "After the person plants the first seed, the next person must walk ten steps and then plant his seed. In this way, each of you must plant your seed ten steps away from each other."

"But why?" asked Jay. "They are just plants!"

"That's a good question Jay," replied Yogi. "Remember the golden rule: everything we do must be done with a purpose."

"But Sir, our trees would have grown and produced fruits all by itself, right?" asked Mariyaad.

Yogi smiled and replied with a full complement, "That is true—you are quite correct. But in a short time, those same trees would have become too bushy, and they would have caused unnecessary problems."

"Ah-ha!" exclaimed Jay. "Now they are more organized and easy to farm, right? I get it!"

"Is it clear to everybody now?" Yogi asked.

"Yes Sir, it makes sense," they replied.

"Now listen to me each of you- although everything is already given to us, we must still thoughtfully put them together for different purposes. Each of you must take a turn and pour some water on each plant daily. Only then they will grow and bear fruits."

After a few weeks, all the plants grew into a small orchard.

"Was that a difficult project?" the teacher asked Mariyaad.

"No Sir, it was not."

"Look here class: in essence, we all co-exist with each other, and also with everything else around us. In our own ways, we uniquely share the same thing. And what is that?"

All the kids shouted: "The Earth!"

"That's close enough, but I need a better answer."

Nobody spoke so Jay raised his hands, teacher Yogi acknowledged.

"In my opinion Sir, if we don't like what we eat, we can change our food. If we don't like where we live, we can move to somewhere else. But if we don't like what we breathe, we have no choice. So I'll say the thing which we share in our unique way, is the air."

Yogi walked over and pats Jay on his shoulder and said, "See? I did not tell you that, but all by yourself, you can put your thoughts together and come up with a brilliant idea."

"So what is our Motto?" Yogi asked the class. "Let me hear you loud and clear."

They all sang, "If we protect the Earth and the environment, they will protect us; and if we destroy the Earth and the environment, they will destroy us!"

Throughout the nation, children were learning different skills and arts. While some were mastering yoga, others were learning martial arts; yet others were training to become scientists and politicians. The whole country was developing holistically. But this was nothing new.

About a decade ago in a far-off country, scientists were already experimenting with DNA and stem cells. These technologies were still being developed and no one was sure about the pending results. A few profiteering pioneers, however, experimented with a test-tube baby. One of them was hoping that it would become a land mine, but when they were uncertain about what the result would have become; they abandoned the project in the nearby forest.

In due course in time, while tilling his field, José — a well-known farmer, accidentally punctured the urn in which the experiment was developing. Suddenly he heard the cry of a baby — a beautiful girl child was born.

The farmer was exquisitely happy and confused at the same time. First, he jumped up and down like a cat fighting with a cobra; then he ran away from the scene like a dinosaur being chased by molten lava. When he realized that he was the only one there, he started to walk back and forth; he forgot that the child was still inside the goblet.

"Oh no, I'm sorry." He quickly picked up the baby and wrapped her in a piece of linen that he borrowed from his horse. Then he looked at his horse and said, "She shall be called *Child of the Forest*. No, no, no.....she will be named *Child of the Earth*.

He turned to the trees and pronounced, "This child will be named after you, Oh forest." He gesticulated.

"Hold on.... hold on, let me think. She will be called *Shree* because she is indeed a goddess. Yes, it is the gods who sent her here as a miracle for me alone."

José hugged the miracle child to his bosom then raised her to the sky and said, "Because you are unique my child, I will ensure that you are married only to someone as courageous and famous as King Omni. You deserve no other than the best of what the gods have to offer." José carefully took the child home to his wife who became even happier than him.

Immediately following this strange intervention, the rainy season began and the land was prosperous with crops. Everyone adored the little girl as a gift from the god of the sky because it is he who sent her here and it is *she* who brought the rain to fertilize their land —about this there was no doubt.

José was not very wealthy; as such Shree did not attend school as much as she should have. Many mature women in her village, however, were her mentors and she quickly grew up to become very thoughtful and philosophical.

Like most young girls in her village, she learned the art of meditation and folk singing. She was different from most of the other children, however. As a young woman, she was noted as someone who spoke deliberately at all times. In the minds of everyone, Shree was truly an inspiration to be associated with.

Chapter Six

Jay the meeting of the eyes

During the graduation ceremony of Jay and the other students, Yogi wanted to impress the guest and members of the diplomatic core about the competency of his now-adult students.

He asked, "Young gentlemen, what do I have in my hand?"

Everybody said, "It's a mango Sir."

"What else do you see?"

"I see mango sauce," said one.

"I see mango jam," said another.

Yogi looked at Jay and Mariyaad and questioned them with his eyes.

Jay said, "From my point of view Sir; I see sauce, I see Jam and I also see a complete forest."

The crowd gasped.

Then teacher Yogi announced to the audience, "Ladies and gentlemen, I now have the distinct honor and pleasure to present to you the graduating class of 2060."

Shortly after news reached the rest of the country about his graduating ceremony, it was announced that José, the farmer at the neighboring village was hosting an event to find a suitor for his daughter. Yogi called the two brothers, Jay and Mariyaad, into his office and informed them that were selected to attend the event.

He told them enthusiastically, "At this stage of your life, I believe that it is important for you to expand on your training to include other social skills. This would be a really good event for you both to attend."

"Can you explain a little more?" asked Jay.

Mariyaad asked, "Sir, is it only us? Why not the other kids also?"

"Well, let's see..., the two of you are Royals and therefore, for you to become true rulers someday, you will have to understand ALL of your citizens," said the teacher. Then he paused and said very firmly: "Thrust me, this is *not* an easy thing to do."

The boys shrugged their shoulders.

"You see, because of your social hierarchy of being Royals, it might be difficult for you to relate to the many different behaviorisms of your citizens. It is pertinent, therefore, for you to endure certain uncharacteristic experiences in life."

"What is so difficult in that?" asked Jay.

"I cannot teach you that my son, you'll have to learn it yourself — it's call *experience*."

The teacher placed his hands on Jay's shoulder and continued, "As you grow older, you will realize that ignorance could be more expensive than knowledge.

54

"Always try to *know* what you want to do before you act; and try not to live your lives by acting impulsively — that's too dangerous! Do you remember when we planted the cherry trees?"

"Yes, I do, Sir."

"The same general principle applies to our whole life. We have to anticipate what the future should be and act on a plan to make it so today. Do you get it? This is why knowledge and experience are so important."

The two brothers could not oppose the wisdom of their teacher, so they obeyed his command.

At dawn the next morning, the trio proceeds gently to the village where Shree lived with her parents. For the two boys, they were not sure if the village was a vegetable farm or a huge flower garden. From their experience in planting cherry trees, this place looks like *'organized chaos '*. When they entered the village, all the young girls sneaked out of their parents' home just to see who *'Mr. Handsome'* is.

As soon as Jay and Shree saw each other, a strange display of courtship began. Each appeared to be mesmerized by the sight of the other.

News of this love affair echoed through the villages and towns like the Headline Story of a new TV show. The whole village was buzzing with gossip.

"It looks like these two have met before," someone said.

"My friend, this match is already made in heaven," commented another.

"To me, it appears that their souls are the same and their bodies are different," said a middle-aged man.

"What! Are you kidding me? What do you know about 'soul' and 'body'? Your wife divorced you five years ago and you can't even save your soul!" said a younger fellow with a loud laugh. "Absolutely not, the gods have *anything* to do with this! Can't you see? That's called the meeting of the eyes man.....the meeting of the eyes, brother!"

Just then one young woman interjected comically: "What nonsense are you talking about god and soul? That's called LOVE you fools, love at first sight! If you don't know what that is, then repeat after me: l-o-v-e. Can you do that?"

That evening Shree dreamt of her favorite fairy. The angel was accompanied by musicians known only to the gods. Celestial singers and dancers of exquisite beauty and charm crowded the sky like flocks of migrating white doves. Shree herself was floating high in the clouds; to her, the moment never ended. But when the fairy placed a red garland around her neck and whispered, *'He is the one'*, Shree sprang awoke immediately, and frantically ran into the chamber where her mother and father were sleeping.

"Mom..., dad, wake up!" She tickled their feet.

"Mom, wake up! Dad, wake up!"

"What is it Shree? Is there a burglar in the house? Are you scared?" asked her father.

"What? Did I leave the stove on all night?" her mother enquired.

56

"No, I had the coolest… coolest — most pleasant dream ever."

"Fofo!" her mom exhaled.

Both parents sat upright.

Her father asked, "So what's bothering you in the middle of the night?"

"I saw this angel! She gave me roses to wear and told me *'He is the one'*. She even told me," Shree pointed upwards, "*I am your mother*."

"No sweetie, *I* am your mother: this is your father and I am your mother."

José smiled.

"No mom, for real. She told me. She said that she is the mother of the whole world, she made EVERY-THING."

Shree's mom shook her head and said, "No love, we all came because something blew up a long, very long time ago. Besides, there is no such thing as an angel; it's all in your mind."

Shree gazed with her mouth open.

"Dad, I know it, I feel it, and I believe it. *HE* is the one!"

"Which one are you talking about, child? Who is HE?"

"You know…the guy who was looking at me today in the rose garden."

Shree paused and then tucked her pajamas tightly below her neck: "He has broad shoulders, muscular arms, sweet curly hair. And he always smiles before he speaks."

"Uh-huh," her dad nodded.

"Mom, Dad, I have this weird feeling; you know, I'm kind-a happy!"

"Ok, Ok, I get the picture," replied her father. "How about you mom, do you have the picture?" he asked his wife. "What are you thinking?"

Shree's mother smiled, gave her a big hug, and said, "Go back to sleep Love, we'll talk tomorrow."

The next morning Jay and his brother were accompanied by their teacher to the farmer's residence to see who would be Shree's choice for marriage. Before any of the guests arrived, Yogi left the two boys in the rose garden and went to José's chamber for a confidential meeting.

The teacher said, "I engaged myself in deep meditation last night, my respected friend. I foresee that my student Jay and Shree will make a perfect couple."

"I had a similar thought as well, Oh learned One," replied José.

"Shall we announce that the maiden has accepted a suitor already?" proposed the teacher.

Shree's mother grasped José's hand and he nodded in agreement. Then both gentlemen amiably embraced each other and departed to their respective quarters.

For this special ceremony, the main convention hall was meticulously decorated according to Shree's wishes. All the decorations were hand-made with flowers from the nearby orchard.

"That's *my* Shree," commented her mom. "Just simple, and elegant."

When the guests arrived and they were properly seated, José authoritatively announced,

"My distinguished friends and families, I am very pleased to inform you, that the maiden has chosen her suitor and she has informed her mother and I, and other elders also, in accordance to our family tradition."

There was uneasy grumbling in the audience, so he continued, "Hear ye, hear ye, hear ye! I want to join with you, this esteem audience, to congratulate my daughter Shree and her soon-to-be husband, Jay—the highly respect and eldest son of the venerated King Omni, king of Ramville."

Many in the crowd erupted in cheers, but a few strong men were not happy.

"This is a black mail," said one.

'This is a setup just to embarrass us," replied another.

"They arranged this whole show even before we got here. I mean how… how can she choose this guy within just one day?" These few mumbled aloud without any regard for the ceremony.

"Hear ye, hear ye, hear ye! My family along with King Omni cordially invites each of you to attend the marriage ceremony of our beloved daughter Shree and prince Jay, exactly five days from today…"

He was pleasantly interrupted by the sound of bugles and drums. The musicians and dancers had already crowded the dance floor. However, only one strong man did not hear the accouchements; he as too preoccupied with his antagonism. As it later turned out, he was the only one who did not attend the wedding ceremony.

At sunset the next day, the trot of horses was distinct when the village horsemen brought the news to King Omni's palace. When they reached the front gate of the palace, it was closed. One of the king's guards emerged from a small hut to greet them. Both guests we somewhat intimidated because, in their village, they saw anything like this before.

"Don't worry, relax." One of them reassured the other. "I believe this is called a *gated community*."

Later, one of the Royal guards reported, "Your Honor, there are two messengers at the gate; they say that they have a special invitation which is to be delivered to you personally. I can report that they have been vetted by our men and they appear to be peaceful and happy. If you command Sir, our guards will escort them in."

As the messengers were escorted into the royal hall, they were greeted with the bang of a huge bell. Then, flanked by their spears on their sides, all the palace guards stood at ease.

"What the heck? What did we do wrong?" whispered one of the messengers.

"Don't look back," replied the other. "Keep a straight face and pretend as if you are serious; we'll be fine."

"Yeah, but what if they take our horses? We'll be stuck here—for life."

"Whatever you do my friend, please, please don't poop on yourself, because *then* we'll be stuck here for the rest of our life"

To their surprise, the King smiled and one of the marshals asked, "What news do you bring for your Highness, the King of Ramville?"

Both messengers bowed and handed the marshal a scroll which he carefully opened and read it.

He announced, "My Lord, this is an honorary invitation from the Yogi, our school teacher, and José, the farmer who found the historic baby in the field a few years ago. The teacher has ordained that Prince Jay be wedded to that mysterious girl. You and the Queens are hereby warranted to perform your parental duties on this important occasion."

On hearing the announcement, King Omni felt a rush of adrenalin like never before. He knew that the educational training of his sons is now over, which means that they will finally be reunited once again. The queens also appeared very happy, but it was Pricilla who jumped out of her seat and ran to the king.

"Do you hear that my husband?" her laughter was uncontrollable. "Our son, yes our son Jay, is all grown up now and he will give us a bride too!"

"Yes, Pricilla, and this will happen in a just few days!" Omni bellowed.

"Oh, I can't believe, I cannot believe that this is happening so easily." She ran over to Kosaler and frantically continued,

"Oh my sister, my son is coming home again! We will become grandparents very soon—can you see? Little ones will be running around in our home. But promise; please promise—it is I who will have to read them bedtime stories."

King Omni stood up from his throne then everyone was silent. He turned towards Queen Kosaler and looked inquisitively. She smiled at the King and extended her hands affectionately. Then he turned to the messengers and said,

"Go immediately and inform the teacher and the father of my daughter-in-law that I, King of Ramville, and the Queens also, have gracefully accepted their request."

The King's senior minister suggested politely to him, "Sir, it is already late in the evening. I think we should offer guests a comfortable place to rest for the night."

"Of course, of course, please make all preparations for their comfort as you see it fit, Oh Holy One."

The King then turned to the two messengers and said, "We are pleased to extend to you, our honorable guests, our humble hospitality. Would you two please have some rest tonight before you deliver this message on our behalf?"

During dinner that evening, the two messengers told King Omni and his wives about the excitement that is happening in their village -- all because of the charisma of the distinguished Yoga teacher and his students, especially Jay and his brother Mariyaad.

"They must be both all grown up handsomely now, eh?" enquired Queen Kosaler.

"I heard that both brothers are very vigilant against crime and injustice anywhere they go; is it so?" asked Omni.

"How is my daughter-in-law, what's her name again?" asked Pricilla.

"Shree," replied one of the guests.

"Yeah, how's Shree and her parents?" she continued.

"She is just eighteen years old. About five feet tall, slim—just like you. She is also a very soft-spoken and selective speaker."

The envoys told them the entire story, especially how mesmerized Shree and Jay were when they first met in the rose garden. The whole village was saying: that was the moment that brought it all together: because that was *'the meeting of the eyes'*.

Pricilla smiled and pumped her fist, "Yeah! That's what I'm talking about!" she exclaimed.

"No one knew about the confidential discussion between her father José, and their teacher though," said one messenger.

"Do you see sister K?" Pricilla asked the elder queen. Ever since King Nemi won the war against the demons and the bond between the two Queens grew stronger, Pricilla always called her "K" during casual conversations.

"I told you," she continued; "young gentlemen have to learn how to *look*, this is very important, you know!"

She performed a brief series of flirtatious facial and eyes expressions. "Yes, they have to know how to look." Everyone around the dinner table laughed.

The next morning the royal servants gave the two messengers tons of gifts to take to Shree's parents.

"These are tokens of appreciation from our King to yours," said one servant. "King Omni requests that you deliver them directly to Shree's mom and dad."

As they return to their village to convey the news of the King's attendance, two of the king's guards accompanied them until they reached the outskirt of the palace.

When King Omni and the two Queens arranged to go to the village where Shree lived, he ordered only five guards to be their escorts.

Queen Pricilla asked, "My beloved husband, would it not be appropriate to take a battalion of soldiers with us?"

"No, it's not necessary," replied the King.

"But why, isn't it dangerous out there?"

"See Pricilla, firstly our kingdom is just like a democracy, we do not attack anybody, nor does nobody attack us. But we fight only to help the good people when they need us. Do you remember the war in which you and I were both helping the gods?"

She took a deep breath and smiled.

"Secondly, success in marriage should not be predicated on power or affluence," Omni explained. "The most important thing is *Equity*. Where there is shared love and respect, there is also peace and happiness."

He held her hands and spoke softly: "We are going to a village Pricilla, not a kingdom. As such we should reciprocate the humility of our host and be respectful of their hospitality."

"But this is a time for merriment and jubilation!" she exclaimed.

"Oh, don't you worry", he assured her. "We'll do that too, but in a simple way."

"Everyone should become the example that they wish to see," Queen Kosaler said. "I learned that a long time ago."

Chapter Seven

Shree's grace

When King Omni and the wedding party arrived at peasant's village, the first thing he noticed was that the houses were indeed smaller than what he was used to. Nonetheless, the whole environment was meticulously clean and simple. There were no crowds or robust activities. He could sense that it would be naturally pleasurable to live there.

"This would be a perfect place for a nice vacation once in a while," he thought to himself.

Just before they reached José's home, they were greeted by villagers dressed in traditional outfits. The locals were singing folk songs while they played their wooden drums and bamboo flutes; it was indeed very pleasing to hear.

Soon news of the arrival of the groom's parents took José's home like a storm. Jay and Mariyaad sprang to their feet and ran to greet their parents with all the love they had. The two mothers hugged their sons tightly and cried so profusely that the Yoga teacher himself began to cry.

"You must also meet the mother and father of the bride; everyone is waiting to get started," said the yoga teacher, composing himself.

While Shree's mother took her to be decorated with colorful jewelry and wedding attire, Kosaler and Pricilla took turns decorating their son Jay as well. Within a short time, there was massive confusion because it could not be clear as to who was doing what. In the end, the wedding parties on both sides were so spectacularly beautiful, even the god of love became jealous. Kosaler looked at the Omni from the corner of her eyes.

"And we thought that ours was an extravaganza!" She blushed and whispered.

"There is a special beauty in simplicity, that's for sure," he replied, shaking his head in awe.

Eventually, both the bride and groom were escorted to the wedding pavilion with loud music, singing, and dances that lasted for nearly an hour. Finally, when the village high priest has a chance to conduct the wedding ceremony, he did so according to the custom of the bride's family. In front of all the distinguished guests, he asked jay,

"Do you take this bride to be your wedded wife?"

"Yes, I do," Jay replied.

"Do you take this man to be your wedded husband?" he asked Shree.

"I do take this handsome man…"

"No, no," the priest interjected. "Repeat after me— I declare before man and God…"

"I declare before man and God," Shree repeated.

"That I Shree, take this man on this day to be my wedded husband…"

"That I Shree, take this man on this day to be my wedded husband…"

"For love and for joy…"

"For love and for joy…"

"In happiness and in sorrow…"

"In happiness and in sorrow…"

"Until death do we part…"

"Until death do we part."

The audience erupted in cheers, then the singing and dancing began. The party was so loud that no one could hear their voices. Pricilla leaned over to the bride and whispered in her ear,

"Congratulations! Shree, you will be the queen of Ramville someday."

After spending a few days with the bride's family and other villagers, the Royal family returned to Ramville with grace and glamour as never been seen before. The bride and groom looked stunning. Some say that even heaven on a clear summer night was no match for their beauty.

Within just one month after their return, the cabinet members of the King's legislator voted unanimously to designate Mariyaad as their foreign ambassador. The king knew that this vocation would take his second son away from home for extended periods, but he was not bothered. He felt assured and completely happy that Jay will be by his side, if necessary.

One day while Omni and Kosaler were sitting in their chamber, he happened to glance into the mirror.

"Ooh! I think it's time for me to write a Will for the continuation of my throne."

"Well," said Kosaler. "We are not getting any younger, but I'm not sure though that a written-Will is the right way to do it."

"And how do you come to this conclusion?" Omni asked.

"Let's say for a moment that your monarchy has to be entrusted suddenly unto a successor, OK? Would such a person have the skill to be effective immediately, especially if there's a crisis? Shouldn't there be some kind of training for these kinds of things?"

"Probably... Maybe then, the best thing is to delegate someone sooner than later; so that I can still function in the shadows, more like in a training position or so ... you know what I mean?"

Queen Kosaler nodded in agreement.

After a few days, Omni mentioned to both of his Queens that he had decided for the coronation of Jay to ascend the throne as his successor. Within hours of their discussion, the news reached all over the kingdom. Everyone was happy about it; Eva however, became strangely perplexed. In her sadness, she started to think of all and anything that could be the result of such change is authority.

"I get it," she surmises. "This could mean only one thing — that I will eventually become a junior servant."

In her agitation, she gesticulated uncontrollably, crisscrossing her room as if she had forgotten that she was desperately looking for something.

As always, the gods in heaven were mindful of any possible enemy of King Omni. They had a strange feeling about the vibrations that were emanating from Ramville when they saw a tiny puff of funnel cloud hovering over the king's palace.

"That's not a good sign," Ezekiel, the chief god, said to his junior — Rudolph.

"What do you see that I don't? "asked Rudolph.

"I can tell that she is not happy."

"How can you tell?"

"Because the general principle is that anyone who is not happy always sees situations as problems."

Both Ezekiel and Rudolph sigh helplessly.

"What do we do?" asked Rudolph.

"Not much," replied Ezekiel. "As gods we only create, we do not manipulate."

Eva walks randomly into her room.

"They say that a strong woman must take charge of herself," she continues to mumble. "If that little swine who was born in a mud pit, ever believes that *she* can come here and take over *our* lives, she is dead wrong!" She thumped her cane on the floor.

"Ha, she is not even wise enough to fool me." She boasted, as she looked into the mirror and slapped her chest. "It is *I*... yes me, who is smarter, wiser, and have more experience than her."

Later that evening Eva abruptly goes to meet Pricilla in her chamber; she is visibly upset as she wobbles into the room. The Queen was surprised to see her because no formal meeting was arranged.

"What's the problem Eva, did you have an accident?" Pricilla asked. "Your hair is looking horrible! Even your cane looks shorter; is it broken?"

Eva walked to the window, stared in silence – she just frowned.

"Come on, speak to me. What is the problem?"

"Your Highness, my heart is broken; it's not my cane, it's my heart."

"But everything was OK yesterday, wasn't it? "What...? Do you love somebody that I'm not aware of?" she chuckled.

Eva looked at the queen and moped.

"Ma'am, I am not concerned about myself," she replied. "I am very worried about Mariyaad – your son. I am beginning to feel very sorry for you, my fair lady."

Pricilla gasped. "What about him? Is there bad news from aboard? Is the King hiding something from me? What about him?"

"Open your eyes- open your eyes, my child! Can't you see what is going on?"

"What is going on, Eva? Nothing is going on. Look... everybody is happy. You are the only one who is acting up!"

"I am acting up because I feel sorry for you, ma'am. You are young and you think all is jolly now, but wait and see that will happen very soon." She wobbled a few steps forward.

"I say to you ma'am, I am an old woman and I've seen a lot. Stop being childish and think... not about yourself, but for your own child. If *you* don't stand up and represent him, who will?"

"What are you talking about Eva? Where do you get these crazy ideas from?" Pricilla appeared perplexed as never before.

Eva walked over to the Queen's bed and sat. The funnel cloud which Ezekiel saw swooshed past the queen's room window with a burst, but neither woman noticed. Eva was confident that she'd gotten Pricilla's attention.

"See? This is how immature you are. What is the point of having a child when you can't take care of him?"

"Eva, he is a grown man! He is educated; he is an ambassador for our country. Why would he, for God's sake, need mommy with him?"

"Oh Queen, he doesn't need your advice; he just needs your love. Do you know? Like from mother to child? That's what I'm talking about."

Dejection begins to come upon Pricilla. She stood in front of her maid and spoke softly.

"Mother, you have always been my most trusted friend. You know that, right?"

Eva nods in agreement. That's exactly how she wanted the conversation to go.

"If you foresee anything which I don't, is it not your duty to guide me...like your own child?"

"Of course my darling, that's why I'm here...to help you and to show you the way."

"Well, then why hesitate? Tell me, please...what is the problem with my son."

Eva became tactfully graceful.

"Your son will never, ever, become the king of this beautiful land. This means *you* will cease to be Queen Mother. How will you account to your ancestors that you failed to promote *his* interest: the best interest of your own son?"

Pricilla froze for a moment as she gazed at the ceiling. "My son... Jay? Mariyaad, which one? Wait, they are both my sons! What are you talking about? I don't understand."

"But to whom did *you* give birth? And whom must *he* look up to? Who is there to show him *'motherly love'*?"

"Eva, stop. Please stop—this is very confusing. Go, please go. I need time to think." Pricilla sat on her chair and panted like a frightened deer.

As the evening went by, she planned a workable solution which she mumbled aloud,

"I will write the names of these boys on a few strips of tiny papers which nobody could see. Then the king will put them in a hat, and Kosaler will pull to see whose name is drawn to win the prize." She shrugged in agreement with herself.

"OR, he can delegate Jay for ambassador assignment for a few years, because he already has a companion to help with the extra workload. I will suggest this idea to the King tomorrow."

As the hours passed, Pricilla became more restless and she could not sleep. She rushed out of her chamber and hurried over to the king's quarter, passing Queen Kosaler in the corridor on her way.

"At this time in the night? Where are you going? Where's the hurry?" Kosaler asked.

"I have to go talk to Omni," Pricilla snapped. "This is between husband and wife; can't I have a private moment of my own?"

"Ooh!" Kosaler rolled her eyes, as she covered her mouth and hurried to her room.

Omni turned around on his chair when his room door closed forcefully with a shove. There Pricilla stood as if she just ran out of a burning house; her hair disarranged and her shirt half-undone. She blew a curl that was hanging over her nose then she threw one over her shoulder.

"Are you heading to the shower?"Omni put his pen into his diary and humored.

"No, I have something to talk about, so we have to talk now," she replied forcefully.

"Okay, this must be some serious stuff, so shoot."

"In just two days, Jay will be crown king of Ramville..."

"Yeah..."

"Do you really think that that's the right thing to do? Did you ever consider appointing Mariyaad instead?"

"Jay is the elder, isn't he?" Omni seemed confused.

"No, no; they were born the same day."

"Uh..."Omni was trying to gather his thoughts.

She held his hands. "My husband, if you never thought of it, then I have a suggestion."

"Of course, I am very pleased that you do have a suggestion." He looked into her eyes with a smile and said, "Usually everybody gives you suggestions, so I am very happy to hear what is yours today!"

She pulled out a handful of tiny wiggly papers from her coat pocket and put them on the dresser.

"These are the names of the boys," she assured him. "What if we put these in a hat and pull to see who should get this opportunity? That would be fair, won't it?"

"HAHAHAHA. No, no. That's not how it works," he held her shoulder and said. "You don't run a country by taking chances — to so requires a very strategic process..." he tried to inform her.

"Okay, how about if we make Jay the foreign ambassador instead. Just for a few years..."

"Pricilla, my dear," Omni spoke deliberately. "It does not matter — *six of one is half a dozen of the other*! They are both *OUR* sons! Are they not?"

"Yes *you* have two sons; I have only one ..."

"That is ridiculous. Come on! From where do such foolish thoughts come into your head?" Omni gets up from his chair and scampers around the room like a chicken looking for its eggs. "Do you even consider what people will say when they hear such an outrageous thing?"

"I know you'd say that! You are more concerned about people out-there than me in-here."

"I am a public servant, hun! That doesn't mean that I care for you any less! You know that, right?"

"Okay, I get it. If you really care for me, then it is *my* request that Mariyaad is crown prince, and Jay and Shree to leave the country for ten years or so, to represent the kingdom overseas."

Omni's knees buckled as he fell on his butt.

"Wa-wa-wa-wa-what was that?" He said shivering, his eyes dilated as he stared pointlessly around the room.

The loud crack of thunder appeared to have come from just ten feet away. Violently the twister swooshes past the king's palace and the sky flashed on the horizon, as a few more vultures peered down over the kingdom of Ramville.

"That's not a good sign," Rudolph, "I don't like what I see," Ezekiel folds his arms and said.

"What do you see that I don't? "asked Rudolph.

"The vibrations which I'm having are too negative."

"Why not, he's the king, isn't he?"

"That's the problem, Rudolph. For everybody else, he's the king, but for her, he's a husband. And if she's not satisfied and happy, it would be most distracting and counterproductive to his kingship. "

Rudolph scratches his head. "Don't these things between husbands and wives happen every day?"

"Yes, but it shouldn't. Rudolph, I say to you without fear of contradiction: when someone listens with the ears of others, speaks with the mouth of others, sees with the eyes of others, and thinks with the head of others—in ways as she's doing right now, they lose their right to be called *'civilize'*."

Ezekiel turns a few pages of his diary and said:

"Do you realize that we've been working for the last fourteen billion years, and it took us nearly three billion years, *yes sir* — THREE BILLION… just to get her to walk on two feet? And in the brief moment in space and time which she's got, she did that! Can you appreciate why I'm confused?"

"I don't know… some things only humans can do, I suppose."

Pricilla reached and squeezed the King's hand tightly. "Are you okay?" she asked.

Omni panted and then held on to his chest. He sweated profusely as he motioned for a drink of water. Then he took three sips then he said, "Yes I am, I'm fine."

When he was relaxed after a brief moment, he held the Queen's hand into his. "Pricilla, to send Jay on ambassadorial duties for ten years is very unacceptable. You know that, right?"

She looked the other way and in a stone-hearted manner said, "Do you remember you had promised me that you will fulfill any wish I ever have?"

Remorsefully, Omni replied, "Yes I do."

"This is my desire Oh king that Mariyaad must be crown King of Ramville and Jay should serve his duties outside the country until the end of the…"

"Oh, I cannot stand this harassment!" Omni interjected. "Do you consider the repercussions of your action? What will your son—as you said it—think if or when he knows that his mother is being combative in an insensible way for what she perceived to be his happiness?"

Pricilla glanced at him from the bottom of her eyes. "I actually…"

"Prici, what example are you setting for your son? How could this be explained to our citizens?"

"I am a mother, I should know…"

"Stop!" he shouted. "You are being silly, no—not silly, but stupid. Listen I can't think for you, you have to think for yourself. So take some time and think it over."

"It's not me who has the problem, Sir—it's you. You are the one who's thinking about other people and not about your family. You are a showman, you are pretentious and narcissistic."

"Leave me alone, Okay. You are ruining our relationship, our marriage, our entire kingdom; do you know that?" he walked backward and sat on his couch.

"So, is this what it comes down to? Are you now taking back your promise? Are you being a chicken? Stand up like a man," she taunted him.

He turned around and bruxed.

"I love you Pricilla, but I don't understand where this stupid behavior came from; you are being such a bloody jerk, it's not even funny."

He approaches her fighting back anger. "Listen, woman, leave me alone okay; you don't know who I am, so let me tell you — right here, right now!"

He stepped away then looked at her squarely, "It is in *my* genes to die with honor, rather than to be a coward and take my word back. In the home where I grew up, we didn't go to the tailor to look good; our exemplary character alone told it all. The entire world holds me in high esteem; they know me as a man of high discipline and of good culture, Okay? So you, yes you, will not come here — in my house — with your god-damn attitude and pull me down. Do yourself a favor and get out! Go! Leave me alone, I will figure it out!"

She twirled like a top and snapped, "Okay, fine."

"And go brush your teeth while you're at it, comb your hair too," he giggled, "because you look like a damn witch right now."

The King's good nature always seems to dictate his moods; but by how Pricilla marched out of the chamber, it is obvious that she did not take the comment on her beauty and charm lightly. That, however, did not stop Omni from mumbling something with his eyes. Even the devil would run away from the look of his face right now.

Later that evening, he went to her chamber to reconcile, but her demeanor was no different from earlier. She did not get up to receive the King. Nonetheless, he affectionately spoke to her as he usually does.

"Pricilla, I apologize if what I said offended you. In the spur of the moment, I spoke and acted out of haste, and for that, I'm truly sorry."

"How many times are you going to apologize for not doing the right thing?" she snapped.

"Prici, we are n adults. We should be thoughtful of what we do. In addition, we are the leaders of this country; as such we need to lead by example."

"Is abandoning your son and wife a good example?"

"Can we at least sit and have a civil conversation about what's bothering you? What would the citizens of Ramville say when they find out that their leader is living in turmoil in his own home?"

"There is nothing to talk about Omi, time is running out."

"Pricilla, it's strange that I can fight daemons, but I cannot fight with you. I don't know what I'll say to our children when they ask about this improvised situation that has come upon us."

Said Ezekiel to Rudolph, "Sometimes wise people build bridges by which even ants could cross the river, but those same ants can also kill a large tree that survives tornadoes and forest fires."

"Yes, I agree. Silently the pest nibbles its way to the heart of its prey and soon even giants would crumble."

"Rudolph, all beings exist and perform according to their nature, but only humans have total control over their choices. That is something neither you nor I can change."

Pricilla said, "If you cannot speak, then I will—it takes a strong woman to make tough decisions."

When Jay came to his father's chamber the next morning, he knew that something was not right. The sheer disarray of stuff all over the room was enough to tell him that there was a commotion of some sort. None of the King's ministers knew about it either; but when he asked his mother about what was going on, she just said,

"Stuff happens sometimes."

"What did you say to him to make him upset?" he quizzed her.

"It wasn't me Hun, speak to your aunty Pricilla." Kosaler did not appear too concerned, probably because she must have seen this behavior before.

"Do you see what I see Rudolph?" asked Ezekiel. "Do you hear what I hear?"

"No my lord, what has come to your attention?"

"More vultures are hovering over the palace of King Omni, and I see many more in the distance. Even the god of the sky is weeping so profusely that the drains and culverts are overflowing. Look, the funnel cloud is swooshing and swirling, just like the King's chariot. All the while, donkeys are braying and wolves are howling when the moon is still hiding. I feel upset in my stomach, Rudolph, I truly do!"

As they spoke, they did not see when Pricilla entered the room; she was quiet as a mouse and stood like a rock. She just listened and stared at everyone from the bottom of her eyes.

"Dad appears very depress, aunty Prissy, did you say anything to upset him?" Ever since he was a toddler Jay called her '*aunty Prissy*' instead of Pricilla, and over the years they became very fond of each other because they keep exchanging fun pet names from time to time.

"Jay, your father made a promise to me which he doesn't want to keep," she said forcefully. "That is the problem."

"Ah! You know dad, he's losing his memory." He smirked. "And what is your request if I may ask?"

"All I asked, is that Mariyaad be given a chance to rule for a while and you perform your duties abroad," she said boldly. "Just for a few years, just only ten years, that's all!"

He stroked her head gently and said, "Don't you worry mom, I'll be delighted to do that. When you are happy, I'm happy too, remember?"

Jay turned to his father and said, "Dad, you are renowned throughout the world for your honesty, love, and discipline. It would be unbecoming of you to take your word back or any promises which you made. Aunty Prissy is right, you can't do that to her!"

He stands next to Pricilla and continues, "Tomorrow, Shree and I will leave for abroad. This way, my dear brother Mariyaad, will have a chance to perform his duties towards you and my father."

On hearing these words of her son Jay, Queen Kosaler slumped in her chair. "You cannot do that my son, what about me?" she cried with her hands over her face. "Am I not your mother too? Does anybody pay attention to *my* wishes and my grief?"

"Ma, please don't do this!" Jay interjects and pats her back. "I know you are a much-respected person yourself. The whole world knows about the tremendous support which you give to your family. I know you can do this mother, yes you can! I will be away just for a short time only. You can help me to make my father happy."

Unaware of what was happening; Shree enters the king's chamber rather affectionately in her unique style.

"What about Shree, what is she going to do?" Kosaler continued, "She is just a young child, so tender and loving. She is so pure and innocent; what has she done for her marriage to be jeopardizing like this?"

Jay stepped over to King Omni and held his shoulder.

"Ma, Aunty Prissy, everybody is speaking about their issues, but what about him? Does he not deserve your support and understanding also?

"Would it be fair for the whole world to say that he surrenders to a lady forfeiting his prestige and integrity?"

"How can a king rule if he is not respected among his own family? What will happen to the state of Ramville?"

Kosaler signals Shree to go to her, then she gives her a tight hug and says, "My loving daughter Shree, you are as dear to me as my own life; I don't want to lose you! Although my son Jay is resolute and disciplined, he is also very—very stubborn. Please say something—anything to prevent us from losing him. Him being even one day away from me again will be too long, much less ten years."

Shree reflected on the wisdom which she acquired during her formative years from the company of mature and experienced women in her village.

"What will my parents say if my marriage ended in disaster? What will happen to the proclamation which my father made to the gods when I was born?"

With folded hands, she bows to Queen Kosaler and Queen Pricilla, then stood beside her husband and said,

"It is with the utmost respect that I say to you my dear mothers — you are well respected and honored for your fidelity to you marriages; would any of you advise *your* daughter to break *her* marriage vows? "

Pricilla stood stone-faced as Kosaler and Omni glanced at each other and smiled faintly. They hope that Jay will change his mind.

Shree turned to Jay held his palm and said,"When we joined our souls together in front of men and god dear my husband, my solemn promise to you was, *'For love and for joy, in happiness and in sorrow, until death do we part'*.

Then she sighs and asked, "Will you take me with you Jay?"

She slowly walked and stood between the two queens and said, "If you leave me here, my love, this body of mine will stay behind but my soul will go with you. As your father, I too am prepared to give up my soul but not my word!"

She turned around and hugged him, looked into his eyes, and continued, "What is your choice, my husband?"

After Shree spoke, the silence that followed was deafening, to say the least; they were all hoping for someone to open the pressure relief valve. Then when the lone applaud came from the corner of the room, everyone sighed so hard that the window curtains flew gracefully like a victory flag. They were all relieved to see Yogi, the yoga teacher, in their presence — they were hopeful that his usual guidance and thoughts of wisdom would diffuse the situation for everyone's benefit.

"Bravo! Well said my child, well said," Yogi applauded. "That was beautifully said — *that* is what the gods call an example of *'elevated and pure knowledge'*. And coming from a person so young yet so proficient is what I call *divine*."

He deliberately moved to the center of the room then everyone offered their cordial respects according to the tradition that was established by the King. After they took their respective seats, he spoke to Shree directly.

"Shree, I proclaim today that, your name will forever be remembered in this world — for as long as men and women live on this planet. You, my child, are the personification of wisdom and grace. Indeed, today you have set the standard for all wives to follow."

He looks at the King sympathetically then surveyed his audience and continued.

"Shree, you've earn your place in history — Ramville might probably fall someday, however, today will be designated by future generations as a day to celebrate your life. My child, I can now declare to my delight that is true: '*Whatever action is performed by a great lady, others will follow in her footsteps. And whatever standards she sets by example, the entire world will pursue!*' — of this, I have no doubt."

Epilogue

Sarkozie said, "Grandpa told us that shortly after Jay left the kingdom of Ramville to fulfill the promise of his father, King Omni passed away by a heart attack, mainly because he was so worried that the curse of Xhi's father might haunt him to the end."

Ubantu slurped his coffee as if he was in deep contemplation.

"So, what about those lines, in the sand over there?" Lee asked.

"He also told me," said the captain, "that back in time when Omni came here, no one ever bothered to clean up the debris when he left."

He walked over and looked out the window of their camp, paused for a moment, sighs and surveyed his crew.

"I say to you without fear of contradictions, it's true that many more before the three of us might have also gone to that big blue giant over there, or spend some time on that grey crystal behind us, or even go to that tiny, tiny little one w-a-y over yonder; but it's always been clear to me my friends that, as of today, it is on *that* little round blue dot over there — the place from where we came — that's where folks are born and where they go back to die also."

He goes to his chair, sits back and relaxes his feet on his desk, folds his hands on his chest.

"And you know what else I come to realize? While they are there, some of them expire naturally, others commit suicide, but most of the times they fight among themselves and sometimes kill each other!"

For nearly fifteen minutes everyone appeared to digest the story which they just heard. Ubantu and Lee went and stood near the window also. They pointed their telescope in many directions, taking detailed notes of everything they saw in the vast dark space around them.

Said Ubantu, "We can come here or go there and dig all the holes we want, we can even set up shop here for a few years, but our main task is to protect and keep that little blue rock over there — the place we call home." He looked into his telescope once again. "Yep, I stand by what I say, man."

Lee agreed and said, "As I see it, there will be a few more like Shree who would continue to make such effort even more worthwhile, that's for sure."

Another of my favorite book: the Bhagwad Gita

Human existence is riddled with battles of all sorts. Although the outward appearance of the battlefield has changed over the past five thousand years, the struggle for peace, love and success is just the same, both at a personal and community level.

Of all the options which were available to Shri Krishna, why did He choose war? Are there scientific explanations of the Universe according to ancient teachings? Do Hindu scriptures concur that I am a small part of the entire universe? Can any of this information lead to my enduring happiness? Many questions are answered in my commentary of the. The Shrimad Bhagwad Gita. It is an inspiring text that transcends the boundaries of nationality, ethnicity or religion.